Choosing the right person

Five key points for the young person

Henrique Pesch

Copy Editor: Julie Castin Cordeiro

With a lot of esteem, I dedicate this book to the youth of the Assembly of God, because it was through the friendship and fellowship with them that I could develop myself as a person and as a Christian. Their lives have contributed immensely to this book. I am grateful to have been part of such a special youth group.

ACKNOWLEDGMENTS

To Jesus Christ, my Lord, for his infinite love and care for my life. His presence and direction have sustained my family and me. To Him all honor, glory, and praise.

I want to thank my dear wife Francieli who helped in the making of this book. Every day that goes by, I am sure that she is the right person for me.

To my parents Edison e Hilda Pesch who modeled my character and always were an example of a couple for me. They taught me to live, and they always encouraged me to do things that would magnify the name of the Lord.

I also thank my leaders for their guidance, love, and care. Without them, surely my walk would be more challenging. Especially to my pastor Dennis Marcelino da Silva, for the trust and support.

To all the editorial staff, because without their excellent services this book would not have happened.

SUMMARY

Forewords................................. 6

Introduction................................ 8

Number 1
Everything has its time **13**

Number 2
God leads us through Biblical principles **28**

Number 3
God leads us through prayer **51**

Number 4
Relate well with people **69**

Number 5
Be yourself and be happy **78**

Final considerations 95

FOREWORDS

Everything in the Kingdom of God and in life rises and falls on relationships. Relationship with our creator and relationships one to another. This is why the book Choosing the Right Person is so important. It is a timely word for a generation that needs to look in the mirror and identify who they are looking for and why.

Having worked as a Youth Pastor for over twelve years, being the father of five and a teenager (a long time ago) myself, I can say without hesitation that relationships between young men and women are some of the most rewarding, complicated, exciting and at times disastrous things I have been a part of celebrating in Ministry. Keeping their eyes fixed on Jesus and not always fixated on the opposite sex can be challenging to say the least. At the heartbeat of every young person's life is the desire to fit in, be accepted and many times find the person they will spend the rest of their life with. Many young people, followers of Christ or not, will abandon principles, morals, values and beliefs to try to win the affections of those same people.

In this book, young people can see why it is so important to have a relationship with our savior and be able to hear his voice clearly. Without an immovable guidepost, it is easy for anyone, young or not, to quickly lose their way. Through prayer, understanding timing and relationships as well as our own personalities it is possible to navigate through these tumultuous but exciting years. In the end, the principles laid out in these pages will give young people a clear road map to a very complex subject. Read carefully young person and then apply these thoughts to your life. You will be very glad you did!

God has a plan for each of our lives and that plan has such joy attached to it. If we can hear clearly and obey quickly what the Lord is speaking, our personal lives will be enriched. The relationships we form will make sense and be grounded in Godliness and purpose. This is your time young person.......rise to the occasion and stand for something few are standing for today; a life of purity and passion.

Kurt Steinbach is the founding pastor of Cedar Point Church in Maryville, Tennessee. He and his wife Kari, have five children who are all serving the Lord today.

INTRODUCTION

Is it possible that God is really interested in who am I going to date, get engaged and get married? This has been one question frequently made by many young people and teenagers of our days. We know that this is one of the areas of significant influence in any person, and the young Christians is not out of this context, for they also have the need of affection and the desire to be with someone special in a healthy relationship.

Sadly, we have been witnessing the young Christians disillusioned, confused, disorientated in this area of their lives for many reasons. The youth is heavily influenced by [post]modern definition of love. Nowadays they rely much on the current trend of what is romance. In our modern society young Christians are influenced by worldly concepts of love. Nevertheless, the world does not have Christian values and principles which we ought to guide our lives. The Bible says in 1 John 5:19 that "the whole world is under the control of the evil one." This means that everything that is in it is buried in sin. A relationship with someone without Christ will, therefore, be more centralized in earthly and fleshly desires. The world views love as sexual desires that can be enjoyed before marriage. The constant change of partners, unfaithfulness, the 'friends with benefit', among other sinful practices have negatively influenced the youth generation inside our churches, leaving many of them confused.

We can also recall other Christians who are not influenced by the worldly standard regarding their relationship life, but by other motives have questioned the care of God in this area of their lives. One of the motives of questioning God is because of bad experiences from the past. Relationships that didn´t go right and that left painful and sentimental wounds not treated that now leave the person disillusioned and hopeless about being happy with someone.

Others, by seeing the situation of conflict of their own families, especially the lack of good example from the parents, lose hope, for many of them not even have desire or see perspectives to find someone special. There are even others that simply cannot find the right person and it seems that no one interesting comes in familiar places, like school or the church.

However, we can be certain that God cares about the relationship life of the young boy and girl who want to be directed by Him. The Bible says in Jeremiah 29:11 that he has thoughts of peace for us. In Matthew 7:11 it says: *"If you then, being evil, know how to give good gifts to your children, how much more will your Father who is in heaven give good things to those who ask Him!"*

Other texts of God's Word show us how much He cares about it because He knows that this area of our lives is fundamental to our emotional and spiritual well-being. Now in Genesis, God prepares a wife (Eve) to be with Adam. Also in Genesis, we see the lovely account of how Abraham was worried about a girl (Rebecca) that would come to be a wife to (Isaac) his son. The Old Testament also contains the book Song of Songs by Solomon that exalts the love between a man and a woman and important orientations for the youth not to get sexually involved with women that would take you to spiritual failure as in the book of Proverbs. In the New Testament, the apostle Paul also has orientations for the relationship life of people, even though it is more specific for the married ones. Jesus himself went to a marriage feast demonstrating his recognition and happiness for this relationship under the blessing from God.

The truth is that we can see in the Word that God is interested in and wants the young person to have a happy and blessed relationship_life. However many youth and teenagers ask direction from God for many things, but when it comes to their relationships they wish to take matters into their own hands and do it themselves. Many rush themselves in dating, and forget the important principles that we should apply, as Christians, in our relationships, especially in dating, engagement, and marriage. Others, unfortunately, move away from prayer and fellowship with God and the church and involve themselves sexually in their relationships, provoking emotional wounds and then they still want God to orientate their relationship life.

God is merciful and indeed forgives and restores, but he wants that the young person has Him as the real Lord of their lives in everything, and this includes direction about a person that would be beside you. The Lord has interest in blessing his children with healthy relationships that glorify the name of the Lord Jesus. Paul said that everything we do should be to the glory of God (1Co 10.31). So our dating and future marriage under the blessing of the Lord will be for his glory, since there is a huge significant force in couples that serve God together and who are blessings and examples to others. That is why, we can affirm yes, the Lord desires to bless your relationship with someone.

In this book, we will touch on five key points that cover how the youth and teenagers can be guided in this area of their lives. In the first place, we will see that everything has its time. After, we will talk about God leading us through the Biblical principles. In the third chapter, we will talk about God driving us through prayer. The point of our relations with other people in general will also be discussed and, finally, we will bring up the point of you being yourself and being happy. These reflections do not exhaust the subject, but tackles known concepts many times forgotten by many of our youth. This book will orientate and lead you to understand relevant subjects about this so important theme. Above everything, our confidence should be in the Lord and his Word that always wants and has the best for us. May God bless your life and guide your walk increasingly more.

Henrique Pesch

1. Everything has its time

I believe that one of the most challenging things for a Christian is waiting on the Lord. Particularly I have little patience to wait for anything. If my wife spends some minutes more than the considered "normal" time to get ready, I already start walking inside the house; I look at the watch many times until I feel relieved we are ready to leave. In the supermarket, sometimes, I find myself looking at the cash register without blinking, as if this would make her work faster. However, I know that God has worked this all out in my life and continues working. That's why I praise him because I see that He is helping me in this aspect. But, and when the most essential things in our lives, like a job that we dream of, that business that we desire, that more constant ministry in church, dating, the future marriage? It requires a lot more to know that everything has its time for these things than a mere wait in the supermarket line.

What the Bible says

Regarding this, the Bible brings us valuable lessons. Let us see some Biblical passages about the time:

He has made everything beautiful in its time.
Also, He has put eternity in their hearts,
except that no one can find out the work that
God does from beginning to end.
(Ecclesiastes 3:11)

I said in my heart,

"God shall judge the righteous and the
wicked,
For there is a time there for every purpose
and for every work."
(Ecclesiastes 3.17)

So teach us to number our days,
That we may gain a heart of wisdom. (Psalm 90.12)

See then that you walk circumspectly, not as fools but as wise, redeeming the time, because the days are evil. (Ephesians 5.15,16)

However, I want to emphasize the known text of Ecclesiastes 3.1-8

To everything, there is a season, a time for every purpose under heaven:
a time to be born, and a time to die; A time to plant, And a time to pluck what is planted; A time to kill, And a time to heal; A time to break down, And a time to build up; A time to weep, And a time to laugh; A time to mourn, And a time to dance; A time to cast away stones, And a time to gather stones; A time to embrace, And a time to refrain from embracing; A time to gain, And a time to lose; A time to keep, And a time to throw away; A time to tear, And a time to sew; A time to keep silence, And a time to speak; A time to love, And a time to hate; A time of war, And a time of peace.

What the world says

To trust in the Lord and know that there is a right time for everything is not always easy. We cannot neglect that life has become fast paced. It seems that we live in days that the world turns around faster around the sun. Every year that passes, we realize that Christmas is already there and then we remember that the year had just started. Today we really are busy – we are involved in many things like studies, work, activities in church, family, social NETWORKS (that take up so much time!), entertainment and so many more things. With all of this running around we get more impatient with everything. But has the time diminished? It seems like it, but this hasn´t happened. The time is the same. We will always have 24 hours in one day, 7 days in a week and about 30 days in a month and 365 days in a year.

The reality is that the world imposed on us so many distractions/activities in order for us to be able to compete in it. The word of God has already told us that at the end of times science or knowledge would multiply itself (Daniel 12.4). People never had so much access to information with the speed we see today. Television and the internet have really transformed society. News is online, every instant. We want things and we want them now! We want everything like *fast food.* We do not have patience to stay in line for food, for people to like and comment our posts, for nothing. Everything goes very fast in this time we call Postmodernity. If on one side all of this knowledge brought marvelous progress in technology for example, convenience, and many other benefits, on the other hand it left us more impatient, with less time to reflect on things, and with fewer personal relationships. We cannot deny that this way of living ends up influencing the Christian youth that want to serve God with sincerity and who want to get married.

One of the characteristics of Postmodernity thought is that there is no absolute truth and objective to be discovered. There is no interpretation or attempt to offer a truth that can be slighted, but not any one of them can achieve the true absolute position, because all of them are culturally conditioned. This has influenced society's behavior in all the spheres, including relationships. Today the world doesn´t value durable and steady relationship. They say, "If a marriage doesn´t go right, just get divorced and go for the next one!" Easy as that!

The Polish sociologist Zygmunt Bauman describes the days we live in as a "liquid society". He explains that this society does not think in long term, they cannot make their projects last, they don´t have any more objectives. Everything is governed by the capitalist market, wherein new requirements arise almost every day. Before long we lose the reflection to make things last longer, to maintain principles that regulate the family making life disorderly. In this same context, Bauman says in his book *Liquid Love,[1]*, exactly of this lack of lasting relationships, in which people are considered disposable, as if the relationships run from our hands through our fingers like water. There isn´t the desire anymore to cultivate healthy relationships; it is easier, when the first problem pops up, to just "disconnect", the way it is in our virtual world.

And God?

However, God continues timeless, that is, He does not limit himself to time, and he also isn´t influenced by it. When God talks of His eternity, He says, "I AM" (Exodus 3.14). If He would have said, "I WAS", the meaning would be that He was and now He is not anymore. If He would have said, "I WILL BE", it means He is still not what He will be. His Word also remains, through the times, the compass for Christians, of all eras. The honorable writer to the Hebrews affirms that *Jesus Christ is the same yesterday, and today, and forever* (Hebrews 13.8). This same Jesus also affirms in Mark 13.31: *Heaven and earth will pass away, but My words will by no means pass away.*

---

[1] BAUMAN, Zygmunt. **Liquid love: on the frailty of human bonds.** 2003

Modernity, Postmodernity and other historical moments and philosophical theories can pass away. Cultures can change and customs too, according to seasons and geographic regions, but our God stays the same and his principles too. They are immutable. That is why the Christian youth cannot be led by this flow of our days in which there are many truths, that everything can change, that there is nothing absolute, because so is the course of humanity. No! The purposes of God for us and the principles that give basis to them stay unaltered through time! This has to do with salvation in Christ, sanctification, spiritual growth, the last day events (prophecies), our interpersonal relationships, among others.

He has dominion over everything and continues sovereign in everything. That is why, in the biblical passage from the beginning of the chapter in Ecclesiastes 3:1-8, the wise King Solomon, inspired by God, wrote that there is a time for all things. He already starts saying that there is time to start this life (to be born) and time to end this life (to die). And so the writer goes on to say there is a time for different situations in life.

A time for everything

The Bible shows us how God acted at the appointed time for His people. In due course, after passing through the desert school, God used Moses to go and deliver the Jewish people. In the right time, David was acclaimed king. In the right time, God moved King Cyrus of Persia to allow the Jewish people to return from exile in Babylon to Jerusalem to rebuild the ruined temple. At the right time, an intelligent and God-fearing young man named Daniel was made a great leader of an empire. However, when the fullness of the time had come, God sent forth His Son, born of a woman, born under the law (Galatians 4:4). This was God's appointed time that is the central point of all history - Jesus came to us!

As we have already seen, Solomon says there is time to embrace and to love. However, what many young people do not realize is that there is also the time to move away from embracing. We can make different interpretations of this passage, but what we can certainly conclude is that there are times in our lives when it is not yet time to get involved with someone. The big problem is that we can only see what is ahead of us, but God sees far, the future and the consequences of our possible attitude.

There are people who rush into things and suffer later. And this is for everything in life. Many teens rush into becoming adults by the way they relate, dress, and act. Others want to rush into relationships. The Bible says that the "wise person carefully examines every step he takes" (Proverbs 14:15). Psychologist and writer Neil Clark Warren puts it this way:

If there is anything that catches my attention, it is the fact that two people tell me that they already know each other in two months, and that they are now ready to commit to each other for the rest of their lives. My desire is to say, "What? Do you know what it means 'for the rest of your lives'? It means thousands of breakfasts together, going through all sorts of financial crises, enduring illness and depression, facing all the delusions and maybe even watching each other grow old and lose physical control. And you think you're ready to make that decision after only a few days, weeks or couple of months?"

Wrong time

I remember two young friends of mine who started dating. She was actually a teenager 16 years old. He was already 26 years old. It did not take long before they got married a year or so later. Many people found it very cool: 'If they love each other, they should just get married!' Even though the girl was very young, this decision would already make her a wife, a homemaker, and so on ... all very beautiful ... However, although the boy was prepared to marry, the girl was not. Of course, she still relied on her parents for a lot of things, and more than that, the bonding with them was very strong. And this is completely normal. As much as she loved the boy, she was not ready to leave her parents' home and form a new home. And unfortunately, this story did not end well. In little more than two years they separated. There was no betrayal or some other very strong specific motive for this; what happened was that they were not able to live and manage the situation

Of course, there are the exceptions with very young girls who get married and get along well, usually because they already had certain maturity. However, we must see this as exceptions and not as the general rule.

How many situations in our lives do we experience that we want something so much at that time, but it does not happen and we are sad and feel desolate. But later, when we trust God and reflect on it, we conclude that the best thing that could have happened was just not getting what we wanted.

It was not the right timing, though it might have been a "good" thing. When we reflect on these things, we see clearly that if we received what we wanted, that would not have been a good thing for us. And yet many times we receive something, after, that was much better than what we asked for.

Unfortunately, many young people keep rushing through things and think that they will never get married! So they change their boyfriends/girlfriends often in an attempt to find the right person soon. What happens is that this boy or girl does not find the right person soon and this ends up bringing more anxiety. It is not a frequent exchange of boyfriend/girlfriend that will resolve, but to rest in God and know that there is a certain time, and if you are in communion with the Lord He knows what will be good for your life and will give you wisdom to distinguish it.

A testimony

I remember an entrance exam I did to enter in ESAEX - School of Army Administration here in Brazil. I actually did this exam twice. It was my dream to be able to enter the army as an officer to teach English. The career attracted me, the salary, and the role that I already experienced as a teacher. I gave my best. I did not pass. Even though it was a competitive exam, I was disappointed, because I thought that the job fit me so well.

However, as time went by, and other things happening in my life, I realized that it was very good that I did not pass that exam. If I had_passed the exam, I would have to leave my city for training and probably I would not be back to work in my hometown so soon. Therefore, many things would not have happened in my life that were blessings. I continued working in a banking group where I was and, after all, it was great to have stayed around. I was able to serve in my church in different ministries that I probably would not have accomplished while away; I am sure it would not have been the best for me. There is a passage in Isaiah 55:8.9 that expresses the contrast between our thinking and that of God. It says like this:

> *"For My thoughts are not your thoughts, Nor are your ways My ways," says the LORD.*
> *"For as the heavens are higher than the earth, So are My ways higher than your ways,*
> *And My thoughts than your thoughts.*

When the Lord says that His ways and thoughts are higher than ours, He says that His will and His accomplishment are better than ours. He says that what He has for us is better than what we think is the best.

Right time

We have to trust the Lord has His purposes in our lives. He will not say: "young woman, from now on you can date". But the closer you are to the Lord and the center of His will, the more wisdom you will have to know how to identify situations and times in your life.

Dating out of time can bring harm to both individuals in several ways. In marriage, then, is even worse. Things can even calm down and straighten up after a period of much suffering. But this suffering could have been avoided or at least greatly softened if things happened in the right time.

However, the same Solomon wrote that there is a time to embrace and a time to love. I believe there is a time for the young man/woman to date and to marry, for God himself wants him/her to be happy about it. However, there is no fixed, "magic" age for all. Some get marry in an early age, and some not so early.

One problem I realize is that many young people are overly cautious in this regard, I mean too frightened about going out with someone and getting married. Sometimes it is because they do not trust God sufficiently in that area. Other times they are expecting perfection in another person, which does not exist. Also, the bad example they received home takes away the desire of the young man/woman to marry, and also this spirit of independence and freedom that the world preaches ends up also influencing his/her head. As we have pointed out there is the right time, and hurrying in the process only causes problems, but too much fear, apprehension, can also be problematic.

You need to remember that God has the greatest interest in all of this and He will help you. We will go through a few steps in the next pages so you can understand better. Dating should be a blessing in a young person's life. We do not want to say that the young Christian has to strictly date to get married. You do not always get it right the first time or the second (this does not mean that you have to "test drive" boyfriends and girlfriends until you get it right), but marriage should always be something to consider when two young believers start dating. If a relationship becomes an emotional conflict, among many arguments, fights, jealousy, etc., and suffering is overcoming good times, you can be sure that it is out of the will of God.

To end this topic, the guy or girl feels it is time to start dating or is already thinking about a marriage. How can they be guided so that it is a blessing in their lives? This is what we will see in the next chapter.

2. God guides us through biblical principles

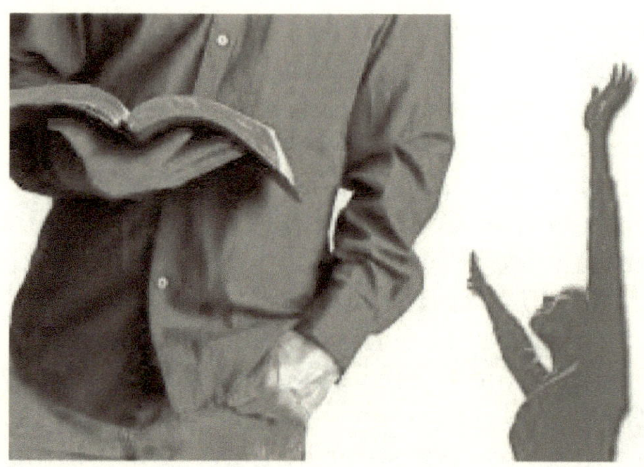

Let's start by defining what principles are. The *Webster's Dictionary* says to be: "ideals, standard of conduct, beliefs". Here we already have a good idea of what we are talking about when we say "biblical principles", that is, rules, precepts, biblical laws. Therefore, they are basic teachings, practical truths that are in the Word of God and must be applied in all areas of our lives: spiritual, professional, family, educational, etc. If human rules and laws, such as the

Constitution, cannot be violated, what about the believer's Rule of Faith?

In Hebrews 5:12 it says:

> *"For though by this time you ought to be teachers, you need someone to teach you again the first* ***principles*** *of the oracles of God; and you have come to need milk and not solid food."*

In this passage of the letter the writer exhorts the Hebrew believers that they had not progressed spiritually and therefore needed to be taught about the principles, that is, the immutable bases of the Word of God.

It is good to note that the word 'immutable' we use is the opposite of what our society dictates. The values that govern our world change according to time and need. If in the past there were not many divorces, well, now the times are different and if the relationship does not go well, divorce! If in the past the believer did not go to any kind of "night clubs", today is different, I can remain holy even in such environments! If in the past the young Christians did not even talk about this "affair" business, come on, everyone has an "affair" and there is no problem with that! If in the past we had to account for what we did to our parents and leaders, today it has changed and I can lock myself in my room and surf the internet right where I want and nobody has anything to do with it! But I remember when a pastor called José Alves taught in our church that the biblical principles are bases established by God for the guidance of human society, and through them man is accepted and relates to his Creator (Romans 5:2, 2 Co 2:8). These principles:

- Do not change with the time or dispensations (Ps 19.8);
- Do not change with space, from place to place (Job 28.24-26; Pv 8.29; Jr 5.22)
- Do not change with the culture of the people (Jr 13.23; Dt 31.12-13).

a) The principle of union

The most important principle and purpose that a young man or woman should analyze when he/she wants to date or marry someone is the **union** or **alliance**. Some texts in the Bible speak of this:

Can two walk together, unless they are agreed? (Amos 3.3)

Do not be unequally yoked together with unbelievers. For what fellowship has righteousness with lawlessness? And what communion has light with darkness? And what accord has Christ with Belial? Or what part has a believer with an unbeliever? (2 Corinthians 6.14-15)

This is the most essential of all issues. Has the other person really given his or her life to Christ? Has this person ever had a real encounter with God? If we analyze the Old Testament God always ordered that his people would not mix with the pagans. When Abraham saw it was time for his son Isaac to get married, God instructed him to seek a young woman from among his people - Rebekah. Now, we who have Christ as Savior are God's people and have to walk with someone of the same faith. Paul emphasizes that a marriage with an unbeliever does not work. Pastor Jaime Kemp says, in his book *I love you*, that Paul, in this passage was saying, "There is not the slightest possibility that they will work together."

Imagine a Christian girl who married a boy who is not a believer/a Christian. On Saturday afternoon, she goes to some activity of her church and stays for the youth service while her boyfriend goes out to some other place with his friends. Imagine a Christian boy marrying a girl who is not a Christian. On Sunday morning, he goes to Sunday School and the wife is simply sleeping at home or complains for leaving her alone to go to church. Even worse, if this couple has children who end up with the mother and also do not go to church. And Sunday night the same thing – each one goes to a different place! This is judged to be unequal! God does not approve this!

The Bible narrates several examples of people who have had marital relationships with ungodly people that turned out disastrous, bringing bad consequences for them and for the parents too.

- Esau with the women of Canaan. The Bible says, *"Also Esau saw that the daughters of Canaan did not please his father Isaac."* (Gen. 28: 8). Even though he knew that his father did not like it, Esau joined these women and brought bitterness to his mother (Gen. 27:46).
- Samson with a Philistine. Even at the warnings of his father, Samson had a strong lust and decided to join the philistine who was from the enemies of the people of God. Young Christians should also listen to the advice of Samson's parents: "Then his father and mother said to him, *"Is there* no *woman among the daughters of your brethren, or among all my people?"* (Judges 14:3)

- Dinah with a wicked young man. Dinah was Jacob's daughter and one day she decided to "go out to see the daughters of the earth." The Bible then says, *"And when Shechem the son of Hamor the Hivite, prince of the country, saw her, he took her and lay with her, and violated her."* (Gen. 34:2) This is a real danger even nowadays when Christian girls are influenced by unbelievers and end up having terrible experiences.

Furthermore in the Bible, we have Solomon's story. He became involved with many foreign women, even though God forbade this union. What was the result? The women perverted Solomon's heart to follow other gods. He was no longer faithful to the Lord and caused a division in the kingdom as punishment (1 Kings 11: 1-8).

Some young people argue that they have seen marriages that one person was a believer, the other was not, and it ended up working out because the unbeliever surrendered to Christ. Of course, this has happened and it can happen because God is gracious and salvation is available to all who want it. However, such cases are exceptions. Pr. Jaime Kemp says that for every case in which the person accepted Jesus after marriage he can mention nine cases where this did not happen and where sorrows, fights, disharmony, separation and divorce prevail. Dear reader, do not take that risk! Do not disobey this covenant principle. If it is not easy even for a couple with the same faith to maintain a healthy relationship, imagine people with different beliefs. And the Bible tells us that once we have made an alliance with someone, we have to keep our commitment, even with an unbeliever! Therefore consider this as a fundamental aspect in your life. I am going to date and marry someone who really knows Jesus, who was born again. That will be the foundation, the basis of your union.

True believer

I think it is very important to also speak about young people who "say" they are believers, but their behavior shows the contrary. When God guides us through this biblical principle covenant, we must be sure that one walks in the ways of the Lord. Therefore, a period of friendship before is essential to be sure about it. Many young people have the false idea that when they marry, they will stick to God. But reality shows us different. Most of those who were not steadfast in the ways of the Lord, before marrying, continue in the same way after marriage or even worse. That is basic, dear reader, trust this principle and God will bless you! What is it to be a believer then?

To be a believer is to repent of your sins, to be converted to the Gospel of Christ, to make a continuous effort to have a clean heart like the heart of a child, devoid desire for revenge, covetousness of others, free from lust, idolatry, malice, greed, envy, jealousy, enmity, wrath, vices, strife, heresies, because the word declares that those who commit such sins will not inherit the Kingdom of Heaven.

To be a believer is to share the fruit of the Spirit, which is love, joy, peace, longsuffering, kindness, goodness, faithfulness, gentleness, self-control. Those *who are* Christ's have crucified the flesh with its passions and desires. (Galatians 5:16-26)

To be a believer is to love your enemies, bless those who curse you, do good to those who hate you, and pray for those who spitefully use you and persecute you, (Matthew 5:44).

To be a believer is to cordially love one another with brotherly love, patience in tribulation, perseverance in prayer. Rejoice with those who rejoice and weep with those who weep. Do not set your mind on high things, but associate with the humble. (Romans 12:15-16).

To be a believer is to not repay no one evil for evil; live honestly, at peace with all men. Do not avenge yourselves and be angry, do not sin. If your enemy is hungry give him something to eat, if he is thirsty give him to drink, because by doing this you will receive the anointing and the virtues of the Holy Spirit of God (Romans 12:17-21).

To be a believer is to renounce every work of the flesh and truly believe that Christ died for our sins and rose again to offer us eternal life. Wait with confidence for his coming to take his church to the holy city, where there will be no more death, no mourning, no pain, no crying, because the first things have already passed.

To be a believer is to love God above all things and your neighbor as yourself, because this is what Jesus said. And contrary to what those who do not know God imagine, following Jesus is no martyrdom. It requires rather the renunciation of worldly things, which makes us much healthier materially as well as spiritually, but it is pleasurable and gratifying to serve the living God truly in spirit and in truth.

To be a believer is to take pleasure in being in the presence of the Lord and to feel love for people who do not know Jesus and somehow work for the kingdom of God bringing the good news of salvation.

It may be that the person you are interested in does not yet have all these characteristics of an authentic believer. It is true that we fail many times because we are still in a process of sanctification, but the important thing is to see in the other person if there is at least one effort, a desire to improve gradually, to be in the presence of the Lord and to let Him work in his/her life. This is fundamental.

b) There has to be love

Okay, the person I want to marry is a real believer! Well, glory to God for that. But I will tell you another requirement or biblical principle to direct you, without which marriage will certainly not succeed.

In 1 Corinthians 13.4-7 Paul says: *Love suffers long and is kind; love does not envy; love does not parade itself, is not puffed up; does not behave rudely, does not seek its own, is not provoked, thinks no evil; does not rejoice in iniquity, but rejoices in the truth; bears all things, believes all things, hopes all things, endures all things.*

There is no better description of love than this! This love is the basic ingredient for a happy marriage. It is natural that it will strengthen over the years, however there has to be love in order to marry someone. However, there is much confusion among young people between real love and feelings or passion for a certain person.

They once asked a young man if he really loved a girl to a point that he would to marry her, and he replied: *love, love, I do not know, but she sings so well!* Any other reason – money, position, similar ministries, beauty, passion – that is the greatest motivation for marriage, and not love, will bring unity to failure.

Love or passion?

It is natural for a young person to fall in love for another person, but one must be careful not to miss the point/forget the objective. Often, what you have is just "romantic passion". Therefore, we need God to not only help us to love correctly, but also to use our reason. Love certainly involves feelings, but it cannot be confused with passion. Many times it is difficult to distinguish among the two, that could lead young people to take wrong decisions which they will only know afterwards that it was not love, but a "romantic passion". If the feelings you are having with your boyfriend or girlfriend vary a lot from time to time, in other words, in a moment you are levitating with passion, and suddenly you are fighting, know that this is only passion. Passion is like this, sometimes you can't even sleep because you are just thinking about the other person, but you might suddenly decide to "take a break" for a silliness. Even if you really like the person, but there are often feelings and attitudes of jealousy, possession, distrust, fights and moments of great sadness, this is passion!

The author Noeme S. Torres says in her book *Only Love is not Enough* that "to love is to have and to give the right to be authentic, free, spontaneous, happy, without needing to hide in the bush to release joy, creativity, sensibility and shared dreams ... it is simply to let each one be, or progressively being, in confident and healthy gentleness - with the certainty of non-betrayal, non-defamation, non-deception, non-egoism, non-envy, no aggression, non-espionage, non-excessive criticism - since each one knows what the other really is."

It is obvious that passion and physical attraction are important aspects. Some call it "passionate love." This ingredient is decisive if a couple wants to have a long and satisfying relationship. You cannot go into a marriage just because someone is a very nice person, or a believer, and you love him so much! You have to have physical attraction. But this physical attraction must be in harmony with other important aspects of the process, because if it is not the relationship it will not sustain itself!

Christian dating

Unfortunately, some do not even consider this term "Christian dating" anymore. After all, what is this? Is the relationship still different in Christian circles? Is it not much like worldly dating and its values? We can say, with much sadness, that many dating within the church, of young Christians, are rather much like worldly dating. The physical aspect has been placed as a priority and the boundaries of a Christian dating have not been respected.

What are these limits? All the impure acts practiced between unmarried couples are the fruit of the flesh. And that's a sin. The following text is very clear:

"Flee sexual immorality. Every sin that a man does is outside the body, but he who commits sexual immorality sins against his own body. Or do you not know that your body is the temple of the Holy Spirit who is in you, whom you have from God, and you are not your own?
For you were bought at a price; therefore glorify God in your body and in your spirit, which are God's." (1Co 6.18-20)

There are young people who think that sin is only fornication, that is, the sexual act between two unmarried people. But this is a big lie that Satan is trying to put in the head of the youth. The above text says to escape from impurity. So any physical involvement in dating that exceeds the limit is sin. Let's be more specific:

- the use of hands on parts of the body where they should not go;
- improper hugging;
- improper positions;
- overly heated kissing;
- sensual insinuations.

The list can increase with everything that we know is beyond the limit. We are not saying that you cannot even hold hands, or give a kind, innocent behaved kiss, heavens no! Excess is the problem! It is to tempt yourself! So, when the Bible says to run away from impurity, it is not only a run-away from the sexual act itself, but from everything that can end up leading to this sexual act. And when this happens, the young Christian is aware of it, because his or her conscience accuses them, their communion with God is shaken and conflicts begin to arise in their relationship. The word of God says:

Can a man take fire to his bosom, and his clothes not be burned?" (Proverbs 6.27)

If you´re dating is in these conditions it is time to stop, ask forgiveness to God and to your boyfriend or girlfriend, speak to your leader and re-establish your fellowship with the Lord. God is holy and demands holiness from our lives. Most of the reasons for the problems and fights in a Christian dating are due to the fact that they are going beyond the limits that God and His word have established.

Pastor and lecturer Erivaldo de Jesus in his book *Christian Ethics in Dating, Engagement and Marriage* describes the phases before marriage as being at a traffic light.

- ✓ **Red signal.** This is the phase of dating. You can not even think of going through the red light. To go beyond the limits imposed by divine principles already carry a divine fine!

- ✓ **Yellow Signal.** This is the engagement phase. There is little time for the signal to open. But here it can be more dangerous than in dating, as they may find that they have more rights to advance a bit. And this is not true. I always tell young couples that "Engagement is not marriage!" We see this in hasty drivers who think they can always cross the yellow sign. But the warning is "wait a little!" That's why the recommendation to the couple is to redouble their care. Do not lie in the right that you can do more now. For those who have waited until now, wait until the wedding day for a pleasurable and blessed sex life!

✓ **Green Signal.** This is the wedding phase. Now you can go forward! Hallelujah! Now all intimacy is released. That is why you cannot have intimacy before, because then you will lose curiosity and grace. So, let's join the campaign: "Those who love wait".

Therefore we can affirm that if there is only passion while dating, there is a great chance that it will lead to a physical involvement as well. Sex is a blessing, but left by God to us to be practiced exclusively within the marital union. Out of wedlock the consequences are disastrous! Choosing the right person is to be next to a person who does not have only physical interest with you, although the physical attraction is very important for a marriage. But the right person for you knows how to respect you and wait for the wedding moment to get physically involved. It is a non-negotiable principle.

c) Character

A third principle that should direct the young person to analyze in a possible companion is the principle of **character**. Would this young woman or that young man had been shown to be a true Christian in their way of life? Are their attitudes and behavior consistent with their faith? How is this person at home, at school, at work, on the street? These are very important questions. So getting to know and having time with the person outside the church will help you a lot to figure this out.

God desires that his image be formed in people, expressing his glory. The Bible gives us the beautiful example of Daniel, who, far from his native land, with no one watching, remained whole and decided not to contaminate himself with that pagan people. I can say, with all the conviction for the girls, that Daniel would be an "excellent party" for a possible marriage! Imagine a boy who is faithful to his God, noble, without defect, good-looking, learned in all wisdom, learned in science, versed in knowledge, competent, with the gift of interpreting dreams, and who had become ruler of an empire! Not bad, isn't it, girls? But what stood out in Daniel was precisely his character, his integrity. In fact, it was precisely because of his integrity that Daniel was cast into the lions' den. This teaches us that not always doing the right thing brings us to 'good' consequences, but we can be sure that even 'thrown to the lions' God will be there with us!

Character involves all aspects of our lives and it is difficult to trust people with character flaws. I always say, especially to those in leadership positions, but this is applicable to all: people will rely on those who do not possess so much technical skill, or who fail to try something, but will hardly rely on those with character flaws. In this regard, even small lapses can be disastrous.

Everyday habits

I like a phrase of the French philosopher and theologian Blaise Pascal when he says: "The virtue of a man is measured not by exceptional actions, but by **daily habits**." Daniel certainly showed an excellent character in his day to day. In the first chapter of the book we see that he and his friends decided not to defile themselves with the king's food. That is, even far from their family and 'church', they knew that God sees all things.

It is very important to see how someone reacts in daily life activities. How does a person deal with money? Is it a person that gives back his or her tithe? Does the person practice offering? Does the person pay his or her bills and is responsible with money? Can he or she use money in a right and pleasing way to God? Has this person shown that he/she wants to have a good professional future through education and work, or do they spend hours in front of the television and the internet waiting for things to fall from the sky? Someone has already said that the "The Devil tries everyone, but the lazy tempt the Devil." We know that many times young people go through tough times to get a good job that pays well to be able to afford his expenses and even more to plan a marriage. However, it is not necessarily how much a person earns, but how he is managing what he earns.

Another question about character is how this person treats others. Is he or she a polite person who treats people with respect and dignity? I heard a story about a certain girl who was totally shocked by the gross and stupid way her "lovable" boyfriend treated a waiter! It made her rethink a lot about the relationship. One of the things that caught my attention when I was still dating Francieli, my wife, was the kind and helpful manner in which she treated everybody, and this began in her own home, for she always acted respectfully and delicately with her family.

Realize how your boyfriend/girlfriend treats his/her parents, how he/she treats the elderly and their leaders. Paul exhorts his son in faith, Timothy, to treat the elderly as the father, the young men as brothers, the old women as mothers, and the young women as sisters.

d) Stewardship

A last aspect to consider in relation to the character of a person is connected with stewardship, that is, how the person manages things and relationships that the Lord gave him. This involves:

- **Time** - How does this person use his time? Is he/she using his/her time to study, work, and do things for God? And his/her free time? Ephesians 5:15,16: *See then that you walk circumspectly, not as fools but as wise, redeeming the time, because the days are evil.*

- **Body** - Does this person glorify God through his or her body? Or is his/her fame of a person who hooks up with different people? *Rm 6:12, Therefore do not let sin reign in your mortal body, that you should obey it in its lusts.*

- **Resources** - How does the person deal with his or her material things? *Proverbs 3:9 Honor the LORD with your possessions, and with the first fruits of all your increase.*

- **Talents and gifts** - Do they use their talents and gifts to do good? 1 Cor. 10.31: *Therefore, whether you eat, or drink, or whatsoever you do, do all to* *the glory of God.* Unfortunately we have seen many people out there with wonderful gifts that God has given them, but they use them only to promote themselves. Our gifts and talents are for the glory of God and his Kingdom, for he does not share his glory with anyone (Is. 42:3).

I know young people who say that only when they have more time, after they graduate, etc., can they devote more time to the Lord and the church. And after they graduate they still do not have time, because now they need to study for exams to get higher in education or job opportunities. And then it is because they are doing a undergraduate ... But the truth is that we cannot expect to have the time we would like to have to be able to serve the Lord. Things happen simultaneously. I have never seen God call idle people; on the contrary, it is in your busy life that God wants you to dedicate part of your time to Him.

Other young people say that only after they make more money will they manage their finances better. After all, they say: "I earn so little! Nor is it possible to give tithing and offering!" But the Bible is clear that one who is faithful in little is faithful in much, and one who is unjust in the least is also in much (Luke 16:10). It will not work it out: if a person does not manage his money well earning little, will not manage earning much. But if we are faithful in the little, and strive, there is a blessing of God upon our lives (Matthew 25:23).

It's in the little things that we prove who we are. As the great missionary Hudson Taylor once noted, who founded mission work in China:

"Something little is something little; but being faithful in something little is a big thing."

Analyzing biblical principles is an excellent way for God to guide us in a relationship. Of course, it would be difficult to find a perfect person in all these aspects, but one must always excel for the best and correct, through God's grace, what is not correct.

As we have said, they are the basis for a healthy relationship. But God can help you even more to find the right person, see the next chapter.

3. God guides us through prayer

Someone has said that prayer is the time when we are closer to God. But why? Let's see some reasons:

- First - we stop our activities. We shut down whatever we were doing at that moment to speak to the Father. This act is a demonstration that at this time the most important thing we should do is pray!

- Second - we recognize his sovereignty. Especially when we kneel, we do not, or rather, we should not do this just as a habit, but as an acknowledgment of the Lord's greatness and sovereignty over everything and everyone.

- Third - we take our thoughts to Him alone. Even though it may be wonderful to be in the church worshiping the Lord, we can sometimes be distracted and our thoughts can go away. But when we are alone with God, our mind is exclusively tuned in to him.

- Fourth - we feel the Holy Spirit in a special way. The Bible says that He is our Comforter (John 14:26) and He intercedes for us, with groanings that cannot be expressed in words, when we do not know how to pray (Rom. 8:26)!

There are still other reasons that make prayer a singular, special moment, for we know from the Word of God that He is listening to us. Peter calls to our attention in his first letter, chapter 3, verse 12, when he says:

> *"For the eyes of the LORD are on the righteous, and His ears are open to their prayers;*
> *But the face of the LORD is against those who do evil."*

Here it is very clear that God is with his ears open to the righteous, but turns his face against those who practice iniquity.

So why does not God always respond to prayers?

It may be that not everyone has an intimate relationship with God! Many people can be active in church, attend it regularly, but even so, there is still a lack of an intimate relationship with the Father. There may even be people who have not yet accepted God's complete forgiveness for their sins.

But how so? Look at what Isaiah 59.2 says:

> *"Behold, the LORD's hand is not shortened, That it cannot save; Nor His ear heavy, That it cannot hear. But your iniquities have separated you from your God; And* ***your sins have hidden His face from you, So that He will not hear****."*

So we have an answer because God does not always respond or guide us through prayer: our sins! If we want the Lord to really listen to us, we must remove the barrier of the sin of our lives that hinders this process. Young man/woman, if you want God to hear you about a future dating or marriage, you need to have an intimate relationship with Jesus, and that only happens when you give up what grieves God.

You may notice that when we pray and start asking God for His direction, recognizing that we are sinners, we ask for forgiveness and cry out for mercy. Paul speaks in 1Co 5.7: "Therefore purge out the old leaven". This has to do with the Jewish Passover when they celebrated Israel's departure from Egypt, but also because the angel of death spared the lives of the firstborn of God's people, and one of the requirements was to cleanse all kinds of leaven from the houses. Yeast is a symbol of evil, so Paul is telling us now in the New Testament that we must cleanse ourselves from all sin and filth. Everything that is negatively affecting our spiritual life must be cast out.

Many young people and teenagers still do not know that in order for their prayers to be answered they must first receive God's forgiveness for their sins and develop an intimate relationship with Him.

A basic foundation

Imagine that a boy named Michael goes to the High School Principal, without even knowing him, and from nowhere asks to borrow his car. What are the chances that Michael will go out with the car? None, unless the Principal is a bit crazy! But what if the Principal's daughter came to him and asked to borrow his car? The odds would be much higher. See, relationship counts a lot!

With God it is similar - when one truly is his child, when his life truly belongs to him, the Lord knows him and hears his prayers. Jesus said, "I am the good shepherd; and I know My *sheep,* and am known by My own. My sheep hear My voice, and I know them, and they follow Me" (John 10:14,27).

When it comes to prayer have you really developed an intimate relationship with God so He can hear you? Or He has been a distant one who makes you even discouraged for praying, for it seems that your prayer does not hit the roof top. If you happen to be in this state, this is the time to make reparation with God! Pray at this very moment right where you are asking for forgiveness of your sins, surrendering yourself to Him again and the Lord will surely be pouring out his wonderful presence in your life. In this way, the channel of your prayers will go up to heaven and will be open again.

Seven Secrets of Answered Prayer

When Moses prayed, the Red Sea divided. When Elijah prayed, fire came down from the heavens. When Daniel prayed, an angel closed the lions' mouths. When Ana prayed, she received a son. The Bible presents us with many accounts of answered prayers. And it recommends prayer to us as the way to get a hold of God's infinite power. Jesus promises:

If you ask anything in my name, I will do it (John 14:14).

Still, some prayers do not seem to have been noticed. Why? Here are seven principles that will help you pray more efficiently:

1) Stay connected to Christ

If you abide in Me, and My words abide in you, you will ask what you desire, and it shall be done for you (John 15:7).

When we prioritize our relationship with God and maintains fellowship with Him, we will be listening and seeking answers to our prayers that would otherwise go unnoticed.

2) Maintain trust in God

And whatever things you ask in prayer, believing, you will receive." (Matthew 21:22)

Believing or having faith means that we are truly waiting for our heavenly Father to meet our needs. If you are worried about your lack of faith, remember that our Savior performed a miracle on behalf of a man who cried out in despair:

"I believe; help my unbelief!" (Mark 9:24)

Focus yourself only on the exercise of your faith that you ALREADY have; do not worry about the faith you STILL DO NOT have.

3) Humbly submit to the will of God

Now this is the confidence that we have in Him, that if we ask anything according to His will, He hears us (1 John 5:14).

Remember that God wants to teach us something about prayer, besides giving us things. So sometimes He says "Yes" and sometimes He says "No"; sometimes He leads us in a different direction. Prayer is a way of getting more and more intimate with the will of God. We need to be sensitive to God's answers and learn from them.

Keeping track of specific requests and responses received is very helpful.

The Holy Spirit will help you ask correctly, *because He makes intercession for the saints according to the will oj God* (Romans 8:27). Remember that our will would always be the same as God's will if we could see what He sees. We need to remember that Jesus himself respected the Father's will (Mt 26.39,42,44).

4) Wait patiently on God

I waited patiently for the LORD, And He inclined to me, And heard my cry. (Psalms 40.1).

The main point here is to keep your mind on God, to keep your focus on the solution He gives. And do not ask for God's help in a moment, and the next minute you try to drown your sorrows in some pleasure. Wait patiently for the Lord; we need this discipline a lot in our lives. God's timing is not our time; he always arrives at the right time with our blessing, for he knows all things and knows when something is good for us.

5) Do not cultivate some sin into your heart

If I regard iniquity in my heart, The Lord will not hear. (Psalm 66:18).

Sins in the heart prevent the power of God from acting in our lives; it separates us from God (Isaiah 59:1-2). You cannot hold on to sin with one hand and seek divine help with the other. Sincere confession and repentance solve this problem.

If we are not willing to allow God to free us from evil thoughts, words, and deeds, our prayers will not be effective.

You ask and do not receive, because you ask amiss, that you may spend it on your pleasures. (James 4:3).

God will not answer "yes" to selfish prayers. Keep your ears open to God's law and His will, and He will keep ears open to your petitions.

One who turns away his ear from hearing the law, even his prayer is an abomination. (Proverbs 28:9).

6) Feel the need for God

God responds to those who ask for His presence and power in their lives.

I have called upon You, for You will hear me, O God; Incline Your ear to me, and hear my speech. Show Your marvelous lovingkindness by Your right hand, O You who save those who trust in You From those who rise up against them. (Psalm 17:6,7).

A friend of mine from college always said that God is our greatest need! Dear boy or girl, place the presence of the Lord as your primary yearning that He will surely show His goodness in your life.

7) Persevere in prayer

Jesus illustrated the need to persevere in our prayers through the story of an insistent widow who always brought her request before a judge. Finally, the judge, irritated, said:

"yet because this widow troubles me I will avenge her, lest by her continual coming she weary me." Then the Lord said, "Hear what the unjust judge said. And shall God not avenge His own elect who cry out day and night to Him, though He bears long with them? (Luke 18:5-7).

Take all your needs, hopes and dreams to God. Ask him for some particular blessing, for help in times of need. Keep searching, keep listening, until you learn something of the Lord's answer.

Prayer should be a privilege and not an obligation

Unfortunately, we have learned that if we do not suffer in prayer it will not have effect. Not that prayer doesn't require any effort of ours, of course, we do, and we often struggle against the weariness of the rush of life so we can pray. However, we cannot expect God to guide us through prayer if we do so only as a penance or out of remorse. In fact, it should be something pleasurable when we have the conviction that God is with his ears attentive to our cry. If we look at the circumstances around us, we will be discouraged, but if we focus on the Lord who loves us with infinite love, we will be encouraged to persist in prayer.

"Prayer takes possession of God's plan and becomes the link between His will and His fulfillment on earth." (Elisabeth Elliot)

Elizabeth Elliot was a missionary with her husband in Ecuador for many years. Writer and speaker, she wrote several books about God's care for our lives and his direction toward us. In the phrase mentioned, Elizabeth emphatically states that prayer is the link, in a very contemporary term, for God to carry out his will in our lives. In her book *God's Guidance - Finding His Will for Your Life*, she says she is entirely sure that God wants to lead our lives, but we have to get close to him to walk confidently. And this approach is by prayer.

Dear reader, do you know what happens at the moment of prayer? God is the creator of all things, and He sustains everything and takes care of everything by his power. There are millions of people who pray at the same time and many things that the Lord does, as Jesus Himself said because He cares for even the food of the birds (Mt 6:26). But even with so many things, people everywhere asking for his help, his church crying out, when you pray it is as if the Lord stopped everything and was only at your disposal, for He is All-Knowing! That is, when you pray in the name of Jesus, our lawyer, God is totally focused on you. That is a privilege! And we can pray anytime, anywhere.

Pastor Ricardo Gondim states it well what is to pray: "to pray is to learn to fight and to overcome like Jacob; to wait like Daniel; to be meek like Moses; patient like Job; bold as Paul and wise as Solomon."

Pray at all times

When Paul speaks to us to pray without ceasing (I Thess. 5:17), we can think, "how can I pray without ceasing"? I cannot always be kneeling in my room to seek God. But what the apostle is saying is that we should, whenever we can be praying in the spirit, for God hears our thoughts and feelings.

For example, I'm going to stay in the bus for at least 20 minutes, I'm driving, and I've been in some terrible traffic, I'm walking on the street, I'm waiting in a doctor's office, etc. Well, in all these situations I may be praying in the spirit, praising, asking for His direction for all things, and that includes your relationships.

Do you know how many times King David prayed a day? In four periods: in the morning, at noon, in the afternoon and at night (Ps 55.17,6.6). And Daniel? Three times a day. Martin Luther, one of the most important in the Protestant Reformation of the sixteenth century, said that if he did not pray for two hours every day, he could not do all that he had to do. Apparently not everyone can pray during this time every day, but I think we can do a little more than we already do. And another constructive tip that will help you receive direction from God through prayer is to attend the Prayer Meetings in your church. Do not just want the big events! Desire the simplc, small things, where God will plainly speak to you too!

What does prayer do to me?

I admit that nowadays many responsibilities and requirements are placed upon the youth and adolescents. They must study hard to pass in a good college or university; soon they need to start working; they need to be 'tuned' in with the latest technology; the world imposes that they need to be always beautiful and wonderful and fashionable; parents want to check our progress in several things; they must always be active in the church; and there is still a future marriage: after all who am I to marry? How do I deal with all this? Often young people are confused and do not know if they are going to be missionaries, if they are going to study Medicine or Law, if they marry at once or what! Isn't it?

Well, the writer Charles Swindoll says in his book *Strengthening your grip* (excellent book, I recommend it) that the most interesting thing in all of this is that the first and only solution to the problem is the last one we turn to....prayer.

See what it says in Philippians 4:6-7:

> *"Be anxious for nothing, but in everything by prayer and supplication, with thanksgiving, let your requests be made known to God; and the peace of God, which surpasses all understanding, will guard your hearts and minds through Christ Jesus."*

However, we may already be so accustomed to these words that they no longer fulfill the expected effect. So let us look at this same text in another version, in the Living Bible:

> *"Don't worry about anything; instead, pray about everything; tell God your needs, and don't forget to thank him for his answers. If you do this, you will experience God's peace, which is far more wonderful than the human mind can understand. His peace will keep your thoughts and your hearts quiet and at rest as you trust in Christ Jesus."*

See how amazing! These verses are telling us that if we pray, all the worry, anxiety, irritation, doubts and growing demands will vanish! Also, they will be replaced by a calm, tranquility and peace.

Prayer is the only source capable of turning this inner tumult into peace and trust in God.

How God directs us through prayer

I remember when I became seriously interested in my then-friend Francieli, my wife today. Although I was already attracted to her, I thought she was too young for me – we are eight years apart. But knowing her better, I could see that she was a young woman committed to God, with a maturity to admire – which made me consider a possible relationship. As much as I also noticed a certain interest in her for me, she played hard on me, as girls do many times! So I sought God's guidance in prayer. And what prayer did to me on this subject? I felt peace and the Holy Spirit leading me. I'm not saying there was not a bit of anxiety and tension, of course, there was, especially when I asked her to go out with me with cold sweaty hands in a nothing romantic place – a parking lot of a supermarket! However, I asked her to date also already considering an engagement and marriage very seriously. And so we were praying, and God was directing us. Prayer gave me the wisdom to discern that I was on the right path, and as time passed, I was sure I was.

When we are in communion with God, dear young man/woman, especially in prayer, the Holy Spirit gives us the wisdom to discern things. When Paul says in the verses we saw earlier that when we pray the peace of God will guard our hearts, a synonym to *guard* would be to *lead.* That is, your mind and heart will be led by Christ Jesus.

Prayer will not reveal the name of the person you are going to date or marry, but surely, this fellowship with the Holy Spirit will give you ever more wisdom and intelligence so that, in peace, you can make the right decisions by trusting in the Lord.

"One young woman, a sports lover and given to field trips and swimming competitions, one day sought the pastor of her church and told him that she felt no special power as a result of prayer. It seemed to her that the exercise was of value, for she felt her body strong and willing after exercising, but nothing profited in prayer.

- Do you practice sports daily? Asked the pastor.

- "Six days a week," she replied.

- And how much time per day?

- "About two hours."

- "And do you pray daily?"

A little embarrassed, the girl replied: - "not every day."

- "And when you pray, how long does it take?"

- "It varies. Sometimes less than a minute. Other times, I spend almost five minutes in prayer."

- "Suppose you were a physically weak girl; could you become strong doing exercises one to five minutes from time to time?"

After meditating a little, she replied:

- "I understand. A little physical exercise would not give me strength, and so I will not become strong spiritually without enough exercise."

The pastor advised her to pray daily.

After some time the girl told the pastor:

- "The exercise of prayer produces a faster result in the soul than a physical exercise in the body."

4. Relate well with people

In this chapter, we will look at a topic that some people find unnecessary, but which for me it is very relevant. There are many young people, teenagers, who are good believers, are intelligent, good-looking, have principles, but do not know how to relate well to people. After all, who likes to be around a person who is very difficult to relate to? Even if there are different tempers, personalities, different forms of how you were raised, we can all strive to relate well to people, thus making it easier to meet the right person. By the way, human relationships are challenging. Since the first family on earth, there have been conflicts. As Martin Luther King said: "We learn to fly like birds, to swim like a fish; but we have not yet learned to live as brothers"!

Relationship with parents

In his book *Finding the Love of Your Life*, author Neil Clark Warren says that in ordinary circumstances our parents are the most imperative influences about development in our lives. We learned millions of things from them during the growing years and even afterward. Although in situations in which the parents were not good examples, their influence on children's life is very strong.

The Word of God, right at the beginning in the 10 Commandments in Exodus 20:12, says to honor father and mother if we want to live many years:

> *"Honor your father and mother,*
> *that you may have a long, good life*
> *in the land the Lord your God will*
> *give you."*

To honor is to cherish, to respect, and not to belittle. Also, a good relationship with parents is significant for a good relationship in a date or marriage. There is a thought that for you to know how your future spouse will treat you, see how he treats his mother or how she treats her father;

similarly he or she will do the same with you. That is, if the boy you are interested respects his mother, with love and affection, there is a good chance he will do the same to you. But the opposite is also true. Sometimes it is not easy, but you should strive to cultivate a good relationship with your parents.

Receiving the approval of parents or close people regarding dating or future marriage is also an essential factor in the process. I have seen several cases where the parents were against the relationship, but the young couple did not consider this, and the result was disastrous.

I know a girl whose parents, friends, and family did not feel comfortable about her marriage to a particular boy. In fact, her parents were against it, because they knew it would not work out. But the girl ignored everyone's opinion and got married. The marriage did not last two years. And there was a newly constituted family that was destroyed, plus the two other families of the parents who suffered a lot, not to mention the additional damage it causes to the church and society.

You see, dear reader, parents, may not always be right. There are overly protective parents or parents who want perfect people for their imperfect children, but most of the time it is wise to listen to their opinions. After all, they are the people who know you very well all these years and want the best for you.

The Bible gives us some good examples of young people who have honored their parents. Joseph, after being blessed in Egypt, prepared a special place for his father Jacob and his brothers. Moses, too, preferred to lose his kingship in Egypt and follow the faith he had learned from his parents as a child. So it's worth a lot to think about honoring and relating well to the couple who brought you into the world.

Relationship in your church

We have already said that one of the principles for a union to work out is that of the covenant, that is, if you are a real Christian, it is essential that the other person be one. So that makes us realize that this person often comes from the community or church where you are participating. This also leads us to conclude that a good relationship with the members of this church is significant, especially with young people and teenagers. After all, how do you want a courtship or marriage if you do not even relate to the young people in your church?

All churches have young people and teenagers. And the vast majority have ministries and specific activities for them. Almost all also have a praise and worship group, drama groups, reach outs etc. The events are of the most diverse: youth and teen groups, meetings, study groups, cells, congresses, Sunday Bible schools, camps, evangelism activities, etc. However, there are still some who are not involved in these activities, making it difficult to have a good relationship with their brethren.

Unfortunately, I have seen young people who "do not mix" anyway! The leaders and the others chase after them, invite them, but they, for whatever reason, prefer to go to church, sit in their place, and when the service is over, they go home with their parents. Do not get me wrong; there is nothing wrong with being on the side of your parents! They are a blessing! But if this is being excessive to the point that this boy or girl does not develop a more in-depth fellowship with his brothers in Christ of the same age group, it can be harmful. Apparently, you are not required to participate in anything. Either if you think you have no talent for singing should you join a group to sing! But there are other activities that you can get involved with so you can get to know people better.

I, myself, met my wife in the church in the youth group. But I got to know her better in Sunday School. We began to sit together and talk. I remember even saving her a place next to me, and when she arrived I already waved, all nervous, showing that there was place next to me! That is why I always tell young people that the best place to find the right person to marry is in Bible study groups or services because this person who attends these is a committed one who wants more from the word of God. He does not just want the important events, big celebrations, but wants something more. So, my dear, if you are not yet attending one of these, begin now, for your blessing may be there!

We should respect tempers and personalities, but if you want to go out with someone or marriage from the church that you are in, you should get involved with your brothers and sisters. It is in this involvement, in the fellowship, in the friendship that people get to know each other so that they can choose whether this person is right or not. But how will this happen if the young man or woman just prefers to stay by him/herself, or as we say, "they think" they are much superior or very spiritual to get involved!

Therefore dear reader, your church or ministry group may have problems like everyone has, but get involved. This will not only be a spiritual blessing for your life, but you will also be able to get to know other people better for an eventual choice of dating or marriage. This may seem somewhat obvious, but many still fail on this issue.

Be a nice person

The Bible brings us essential lessons from Ruth's life. We all know her story when she decided to stay with her mother-in-law even after her husband passed away. When she decides to stay with her mother-in-law and accompany her, several qualities of her are highlighted. These conditions were seen by God and men. Consequently, a man, named Boaz, became interested in Ruth and married her blessing her life greatly. In fact, the son of Ruth with Boaz was Obed, David's grandfather, a legitimate ancestor of Jesus. (If you can read Ruth's book to understand the story better, read it, it is only four chapters). But let us look at the various qualities in Ruth in which young people can mirror themselves:

- Altruism, that is, the emptying of pride, of corrosive vanity (Rt 1: 12-15); How annoying it is to be around proud people who never do good to others.

- Laboriousness, that is, a young woman who was not lazy to work (Rt 2.2)

- Affectivity (Rt 1.16); Showed affection and desire to share good things as bad things; people with this quality attract others.

- Faithfulness (Rt 2.18); Loyalty is the main feature of friendship; If there is no fidelity, there is no trust.

- Obedience (Rt 3.5); How sad it is to see young disobedient to their parents, leaders, pastors; but obedience draws blessings!

- Humility (Rt 2.10); This is not to say simpleton; but rather a person who does not consider himself superior to others, or because of his beauty, his intelligence, his possessions, his positions or even his spirituality.

- Nice person (Rt 2.11); We can understand from the text that Ruth was conquering the trust and admiration of the people in Bethlehem. She made friends and this came to Boaz. In short, she was a pleasant person. Who likes to be with unpleasant, annoying person? No one. Even though she was in terrible pain for the loss of her husband, she did not let bitterness overpower her and leave her a closed and antisocial person. She trusted in God, let the Spirit work in her, and for her admirable attitudes of personality, she obtained the favor of the Lord in a happy and blessed marriage.

And we still have the simple issue of ethics! Ruth was a person with ethics. Many young people cannot be nice people because of ethics. Ethics and morals are applied to a balanced life. Every person who has ethical or moral principles knows how to respect others, is polite, knows how to say, "Good morning, good afternoon, good evening, sorry, excuse me, thank you".

We often have several excuses for our bad relationship with people. "It's because it comes from my family, it's because I'm like this ..." "Ah, because the people of this city are really cold ..." "Ah, because in this church the young people do not talk" "Ah, I am afraid to fall in love." Dear reader, you are a unique person who has the Holy Spirit in you. Make your own choices. Be a person who gets along with everyone and has a good relationship with your group. Naturally, if you relate well to people, it does not mean that you will give up your convictions to just "get along" with someone, but Paul warns you that depending on us, we need to have peace with everyone!

5. Be yourself and be happy

People, and that include young people, live making comparisons. They compare themselves with others and compare people to each other. They compare:

- hair
- body
- beauty
- clothes
- culture
- intelligence
- spirituality
- churches

Whenever we make comparisons, someone loses. And often it is us. Imagine when you say:

- "If I were as smart as James ..." (You are putting yourself as a being inferior to him);

- "If I were as beautiful as Pamela ..." (You are giving an excuse to justify some frustration);

- "If I were as talented as that person ..." (You are also giving an excuse to justify some other frustration).

When we make comparisons like these and others, we cannot see how unique and special people are. Every young person or teenager is singular. There was not, there is not, and there will not be someone like you. And God alone can do this, for He is the Creator and made each of us with specific characteristics.

Accepting yourself

For example, you have a specific height, and you cannot increase or decrease it, no matter what you do. Some young fellows even try to walk around with their neck high giving a "big boy" look. Some girls also want to be taller and never take off those "mega" high heels. But it is no use, Jesus said, *"Which of you by worrying can add one cubit to his stature?"* (Matthew 6:27). No one can.

Another aspect that we cannot change in ourselves is our essence, that is, what we really are! And many young people would like to be different. They wanted to be more communicative, or quieter, or more this or that.

It is true that we can change some things from our physical aspect like doing some physical exercise and eating less to lose weight or eat more and work out to gain weight. But fundamental characteristics of our body we cannot change, and so we have to respect it.

In the same way, it is with our personality. Some traits will inevitably accompany us for the rest of our lives. I am a somewhat uneasy person by nature, unlike my wife, who is much calmer and quiet. Naturally, I can control my personality traits, and not use excuses for misbehavior just by saying "I am like that." But the point is that these fundamental characteristics of our personality will be with us forever, and that is what makes us unique individuals. And understanding that situation is the first step to relating well with someone else.

> *Each of us has its essence and wanting to change it is a way of not accepting people as they are* (Roberto Shiniashiki)

I remember a biblical story of two girls fighting over the same man. This happened in the Old Testament with the young Leah and Rachel who fought for a young man named Jacob. The young women's father set the guy up to take for his wife Leah, the oldest and least favorite. The plot was dishonest and bizarre, but Jacob had already given his heart to the younger one, Rachel. That way Leah was on the losing side, she knew what it was like to be rejected by someone. Compared with Rachel, Leah was ordinary, and it made her feel unwanted.

Maybe you feel like Leah, rejected, secondary, out of place in this world. Perhaps you do not have a talent that catches everyone's attention. Possibly you are not that popular, not a girl magazine cover, a student with the best grades. It is possible you do not accept yourself how you are ordinary. But I want to give you good news: God does not consider you average! In fact, he created you special and unique, and for a specific purpose. He did not make you by chance, but he has an all-specific plan with you that will not be the same with anyone in this world.

Self esteem

What is self-esteem?

1. It is what I think about myself;
2. How I feel with my thoughts;
3. What do I make of my life from this...

Therefore, self-esteem is this mixture of visions and judgments that we have to ourselves. It manifests itself through emotions and weighs on our inner well-being, our tranquility, and our worries. It is natural to the human being and influences our way of being.

Self-esteem is a kind of control panel of our being. It shows us what is working or not. It shows our needs if we are satisfied in some areas of life, for example, of affection and love. It manifests itself by two main chains. The first by social recognition: all manifestations of affection, appreciation, the esteem of other people. The second, our performance: all our achievements, acts of success. In this way, self-esteem has a high power in directing our personalities. For example, it makes us fearful or courageous under certain circumstances.

Practicing good self-esteem

Accepting yourself is essential to good self-esteem. For the young Christian, who is sure that God created him/her like this, to like him/herself, that is, someone who God made according to his power, must be a constant.

A specialist in the subject named Christophe André points out five dimensions for good self-esteem practice:

1. Balance your self-esteem: To have a balance on how we think about ourselves is ideal. Some people always exaggerate showing a very high self-esteem. They seem to be unshakable. And this can only be "fake." The very word says: *through the grace given to me, to everyone who is among you, not to think of himself more highly than he ought to consider,* (Rom. 12:3). We are nothing if it is not the grace of God. Others have very low self-esteem, becoming devalued, forgetting that God created them. But as we have already said self-acceptance is essential for a reasonable level of self-esteem.

2. Stability: This shows about the events of life. It is essential for the young person to maintain stable his self-esteem in the face of failures and difficulties. The painful moments will come, but we cannot allow this to destabilize our self-esteem.

Adversities happen just to prove our stability. But we can be sure that all things work together for the good of those who love God (Rom. 8:28).

3. Harmony: It is crucial that the young person does not concentrate all of their self-esteem in only one area of their life. For example physical appearance, going out with someone, professional life, among others. If you do, when things are not going well in this area, your self-esteem will automatically drop a lot. It is essential that you develop harmony, valuing all aspects of your life as family, friends and especially your fellowship with God. That way, if you lose your job, for example, you relativize this by valuing other essential aspects of your life. If you would like to be with someone and you are not, you should continue to dedicate yourself to other areas, without lowering your self-esteem, because the time will come! Having a balance and enjoyment in everything we do is fundamental to maintain this harmony.

4. Independence: This is identified by the independence you have before the social pressures imposed by what you should have, how it should be and what it should do. Usually, this outside pressure tells us that we should have this kind of appearance, have this brand of car, take this course, and walk this way! As believers, we must walk according to Christian principles and not by the pressure of the world. So to have autonomous self-esteem, you must emphasize your inner values and virtues, do not give up because you do not meet the demands of society. I am not telling you to walk anyway you want to and "don't care for anything" to be able to grow and develop, but do not get carried away by the crazy demands of this world.

5. Maintenance: It is necessary to maintain a reasonable level of self-esteem. There are people who make tremendous emotional and psychological sacrifices just to keep good self-esteem for some time. But the young Christian must daily preserve his/her self-esteem so as not to live on a roller coaster of his emotional states. He/she must practice daily prayer, read the Word, trust in God and try the best to practice the aspects mentioned so far.

Be yourself

When we learn to accept ourselves as we are, we develop good self-esteem. Therefore, I know that I can be myself when I am with someone. I know that person will like me the way I am. Again I am not saying that the other person has to accept all your flaws and faults. For example: if you are heated up by "short-tempered" the other person has to take it anyway, and it is over! If you have an attitude, that the other person does not like and you insist on doing it because he/she has to accept you as you are. No! We all have to strive to change harmful attitudes and behaviors that are destructive to others and ourselves. What I am saying is that these changes cannot change the essence of our being and that we must be different just to please the other person.

I met a couple where the boy was very sociable, charismatic, talked to everyone in the church, etc. The girl was also a good person, but more modest and shy. What happened was that she started banning her boyfriend from talking to people wanting his attention just for her. Of course, the primary focus of the couple should be aimed at each other, and both should do everything to please each other, but limiting someone from being himself will only bring frustration and adverse consequences to the relationship. To end the story of the couple I met, well, this situation was not sustained, in addition to other exaggerated demands that she made, they broke up. The couple should trust each other, be sincere in the changes that need to be made, but always let the person be himself/herself to have a healthy relationship.

If you have to change a lot in one relationship only to please the other, you should rethink the relationship. If you feel limited, stuck, always walking on thin ice with the other person, talk seriously to her/him for changes or rethink your realtionship.

God wants to use you as you are

Maybe you are already tired of comparing yourself to other people and want talents they have such as communication, musical talents, being more affluent, and so on. However, the truth is that God created you and often God uses people who are ordinary to accomplish great things for him.

Do you remember David? He was not even the most appreciated brother in the family. His father considered him only a shepherd of sheep, and when prophet Samuel came to his house, David was the last son to be presented. But there was already a plan in his life, and he became the greatest king of Israel.

Rebekah was an ordinary person who went to the well at the right time and, by her disposition and help, was chosen to be the wife of Isaac, one of the patriarchs of the people of Israel.

The disciples of Jesus were ordinary men. Peter, James, John, and Andrew were rude fishermen, without many cultures. Matthew was a tax collector hated by almost everyone in that Jewish society. Historians say that Paul was hunchbacked, short and unattractive. Very ordinary people who have surrendered themselves to God's designs in their lives turned the world upside down and left writings that have become the bible we have today.

So do not worry about being an ordinary young person or teenager, God wants to use you to accomplish great things for Him. Recall what Psalm 139:15,16 says:

> *"My frame was not hidden from You*
> *when I was made in secret,*
> *and skillfully wrought in the lowest parts of the earth.*
> *Your eyes saw my substance, being yet unformed.*
> *And in Your book they all were written,*
> *the days fashioned for me, when as yet there were none of them."*

Prioritize communication

We all know the importance of dialogue, of good communication, to have a good relationship between two people. Communication is the foundation of a healthy relationship. By the way, communication will be the channel for you to know if you are choosing the right person. I remember when I went to live in the United States in my teens, and an American girl named Amy from my school charmed me. In fact, I never was able to exchange a word with her, since I had just arrived there and spoke almost nothing in English. That is, zero communication! But some situations even speaking the same idiom, there is also no communication because they speak different languages.

In the bestseller, *The 7 Habits of Highly Effective People* the writer Stephen R. Covey lists two crucial points for good communication:

- **Listen with empathy:** What is empathy? It is putting you in the other person's shoes. It is to seek to understand first. Most people cannot listen with the intention of understanding. Listening empathetically is not making pre-judgments before you listen and understand. This is very important in any relationship, whether in a friendship, dating, marriage, etc.

- **Understanding and perception:** After you understand what is happening to the other person, your perception is significantly improved. Often we do not strive to understand people, and thus we do not realize how we can develop our relationship. Some young people just want to be understood and talk too much when they are interested in someone, but they never stop to listen to the other person.

Perception also involves our communication through body language. Most of our communication takes place without words, only through this body language, facial expression, and tone of voice among other characteristics. Over time in a relationship, this will become clearer.

In a friendship where there is an interest in a possible dating or in a relationship, communication should be prioritized to the fullest. Many misunderstandings and fights happen not because someone has done something wrong or intentional, but out of sheer lack of good communication.

The dialogue is so fundamental that often in friendship, in conversation, you can already see if a certain person would be right for you. In dating, you should talk a lot more and more to make sure that this is the person you want to spend the rest of your life.

Be happy

How to be happy with someone? How to choose someone to whom I will be pleased with? Even though the subject matter may be more complicated, I believe that the points we have discussed so far will certainly help you choose the right person. As we have said before, many times you do not get it right the first time, or the second time, but knowing yourself and fellowship with God will be fundamental to a correct choice.

However, I have put the verb of this subtopic "Be happy" in the imperative purposefully. This gives us the idea of choice, of taking an attitude, a step toward being happy with someone. Many young people have the misconception that the other person must have the full responsibility of the world for them to be happy. This is a misunderstanding. Many girls wait for the "charming prince" who will show up in front of her house mounted on a white horse and say: "I came to get you, my love"! And a lot of guys are waiting for the "Miss Universe" with no appearance, personality or temperament flaws to show up for him to motivate himself. There are still those who want an angel from the sky to come down and point to the boy or the girl saying, "this is the person you are going to marry"! There may even have been some specific revelation about a future marriage, but as a general rule, God does not work that way.

Not waiting for the perfect person does not mean that I will lower my standards or that I will surrender principles and guidelines that we have studied here so far. To be happy is to be aware that I have flaws too, so I will not expect angels, and wisely, I will make choices that will direct me toward happiness. There are many young people overly frightened today about everything. They never take a step of faith, fear is always a barrier. And that includes starting a relationship with someone. Some young people are afraid even of starting a conversation with another person, friendship, a beginning of interest, because of the excessive fear of making mistakes. But the Bible says that if we are in the love of God, there is no fear (1 John 4:18). Yes, there is fear of God, wisdom, and trust.

It is also important to emphasize that before being happy with someone, you need to be happy alone, with yourself. A good relationship requires two healthy people. Being healthy does not just mean physically, although this is important to care for. And not only spiritually healthy, although this is fundamental. But I want to stress here being mentally and emotionally healthy. There are many examples of young people who start dating and then get married, but the lack of emotional health of one of the two involved is clear.

I remember a couple I met years ago. The girl had a totally emotionally unstable life, especially in her turbulent relationship with her parents. She simply did not listen to her parents and had fights with them often. Nor did she take her studies seriously. The boy was also, immature, from an unstructured family. The two began to date, and soon it was possible to perceive the immaturity of both directly affecting the relationship.

Due to the lack of emotional health, immaturity, stubbornness of both, the relationship began to wear off by fights, jealousy generating uncontrollable passion. But nothing made them give up marrying. And what usually happens when two people in this state marry is that things, instead of improving, they get worse. Soon they had a beautiful girl, but the union did not sustain itself, and they ended up separating. And there it was, one more case of two young people defeated, now with a daughter who would not have the presence of the father in her development, all because of two unhealthy young people who decided to unite.

What I want to tell you dear boy/girl is that you should not drag your emotional baggage into a wedding thinking that there you will find the solution. Over time, the tendency is to get worse, so take care to be a healthy person before marriage and stay healthy later.

Being happy also requires that you, as a teenager, have heard so many times, that is to seek to make the other person happy, but not to nullify yourself and your happiness, but to put yourself in attitudes that will be beneficial to both. When seeking to make the other happy, it is natural for the other person to make you happy as well. In short, choose to be happy, have God ahead of your path, and let Him guide your life, be honest and frank with the other person, make the necessary adjustments, be yourself and be happy.

Final considerations

Every day when we wake up, there will be a day when we have to make choices. We choose what clothes we will wear, what we will eat for breakfast, what appointments we will make that day and if we are going to do anything else. Although many of these choices become habits and some do not require much effort from us, it is certain that life is made of choices.

Choosing the right person for a serious commitment is one of the most important one. I get scared when I see so many unhappy couples who do not understand each other because they did not allow themselves to be guided by God and the wisdom of the Bible and made a wrong choice. But I believe with all my heart that the Lord wants to bless your life in this area, as he has done in mine and so many others. And not because we are worthy, but because of the immeasurable goodness of the Lord in our lives. God knows your innermost, your deepest feelings and He wants to guide you. However, there is your part to do, and what I have addressed in this book are fundamental points that will help you, will shed light on this path. I did not pretend to say everything about such a vast subject, but to point out known truths, but often forgotten by young people and teenagers.

When we look at the world, we are discouraged because it has nothing to offer us, because its values are contrary to ours. You, young person, must know that there is someone who cares about you and wants to give you the best. And with each day that you give yourself more and more into His hands, divine wisdom will be part of your life and will help you make wise decisions. God is interested; He wants you to have a blessed date, a blessed engagement, and a blessed marriage! We see romanticism throughout the Bible: when the Lord chooses a garden for the first couple; the book of Song of Solomon describing love and marriage; and with Jesus symbolically describing his coming to get his bride, the church.

It is in this confidence and assurance of God's direction that I want you to find the right person and be very happy. Even aware that there will be hard times because we are imperfect people who seek improvement every day. I wish that from the first moments that you find someone, be moments of peace, joy, companionship, romanticism, and fellowship. That while you are alone, you rest in God and be happy, and then, making a right choice, you continue to be satisfied with the blessing of the Father.

But he wants you to put him above all things. He wants to be the first of your heart. Maybe it's not the time for you to get involved, or you need to obey fundamental principles to have a blessed relationship. The truth is that when you have the Lord directing this aspect of your life, trusting, and expecting it, you will see His hand acting and guiding you. Trust and rest, our God is a God of wonders.

REFERENCES

ANDRÉ, Christophe. **Imperfect, free and happy - practices of self-esteem.** Best*Seller*, 2009.

BAUMAN, Zygmunt. **Liquid love: on the frailty of human bonds.** Polity Press, 2003.

BIBLE. New King James Version. Thomas Nelson, 1985.

BIBLE. The living Bible. Tyndale House Publishers, 1978.

CARSON, D.A. **The Gagging of God**. Grand Rapids: Zondervan, 1996.

COVEY, Stephen R. **The 7 Habits of Highly Effective People.** New York: Free Press, 2004.

DARLING, Daniel. **Teenagers from the Bible. You are very similar to them.** Rio de Janeiro: CPAD, 2014.

ELLIOT, Elizabeth. **God's Guidance: Finding His Will for Your Life.** 2nd ed. Grand Rapids: Revell. 2006.

GONDIM, Ricardo. **Living in Triumph**. São Paulo: Doxa Produções, 2000.

JESUS. Erivaldo; JESUS, Cristiane. **Christian Ethics in Dating, Engagement and Marriage.** Adib Editora, São Paulo, 2011.

KEMP, Jaime. **I love you**. São Paulo: Hagnos, 2005.

_____. **Dating, Engagement, Marriage and Sex.** São Paulo: Editora Sepal, 1996.

ROBERTS, Wes; WRIGHT, H. Norman. **Before you say "I do".** Eugene, Oregon. Harvest House Publisher, 1978.

ROSA, Antonieta. **Ruth: a woman richly blessed by God.** Rio de Janeiro: Editora Jeová Nissi, 2008.

SHINIASHIKI, Roberto; DUMÊT, Eliana Bittencourt. **Loving can work out.** São Paulo: Editora Gente, 2006.

SWINDOLL, Charles. **Strengthening your grip.** Waco, Texas: Word books, 1982.

TORRES, Noeme S. **Only love isn't enough.** Rio de Janeiro: Editora Adhonep, 2000.

WARREN. Neil Clark. **Finding the love of your life** New York, Pocket books, 1994.

Contacts

@henriquepesch
h_pesch@yahoo.com.br

www.ingramcontent.com/pod-product-compliance
Lightning Source LLC
LaVergne TN
LVHW090132160826
845673LV00017B/2182

* 9 7 8 8 5 6 8 4 6 3 2 0 8 *